Composition 3

Michael Dean

Longman

The printer doesn't work.

Writing a note and a letter explaining what is wrong

Completing sentences

1 **Match the problems to the correct appliance.**

1 It keeps ringing when there's nobody phoning me.
2 It's always playing the wrong song.
3 The paper keeps jamming.

a computer printer
b CD player
c mobile phone

2 **Read Laura's note to her dad, then complete her dad's letter to the printer firm.**

Dear Dad,
There's a problem with the computer printer. The paper keeps jamming. Every time I put paper in the printer it jams. Phone me on the mobile, please. I'll be at Melanie's. Thanks.
Love, Laura

P.S. Dad, there's another problem. Please tell the firm this: The printer's always printing out badly. The print comes out too black. Thanks again, L.

Tip

P.S. means you have thought of something else.

27 New Road
London
13 September 2002

Dear Sir or Madam,
There 1 _____ _____ problems with our Big Boy XJX printer. First, the
2 _____ _____ _____ . Every 3 _____ _____ ____
_____ _____ _____ _____ _____ _____ . Secondly, 4 _____
_____ _____ _____ _____ _____ _____ .
The 5 _____ _____ _____ _____ _____ .

3 **Complete the sentences with problems with machines.**

Tip

keeps + -ing   is always + -ing
The problem happens more than once.

1 My mobile phone is always _____ .

2 Whenever my CD player _____ .

3 My computer keeps _____ .

4 My electronic personal organiser is always _____ .

5 My pocket calculator _____ .

Writing sentences

4 Write full sentences in the correct speech bubbles.

    a What/wrong/your phone?
    b But/I/never/talk/anybody!
    c I/phone/mobile phone firm.
    d I can't hear/anyone!

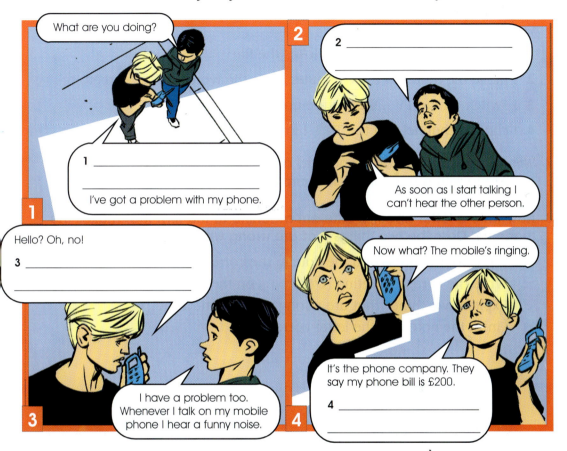

5 Write two sentences about problems with each machine.
    Use the words in brackets. You can use a dictionary.

    1 Video game
(Can't see/game/on/TV) I can't see the game on the TV.
(Mario/always/same room/castle)

    2 Bike
(wheel/come off)
(saddle/fall off)

    3 Personal stereo
(headphones/not work)
(play/slow)

Putting sentences together

6 Write the sentences again with *Whenever* and *As soon as*.

Example:

I start the car – it stops again.

<u>Whenever</u> I start the car it stops again. = <u>As soon as</u> I start the car it stops again.

1 I press 'Save' – the computer loses the file.

2 I move the mouse – the computer loses the words on the screen.

3 I switch on the TV – the picture goes black and white.

4 I change channels on the TV – I lose the sound.

7 Write a note to your mum and dad or a friend describing two things that are wrong with a machine. Use Laura's note on page 2 as an example.

8 Now write a letter about a different machine to the firm that makes the machine. Describe two things that are wrong with the machine.

⊠ Write your address and the date in the correct place on the letter.

⊠ Write the correct greeting (*Dear* . . .) on the note and the letter.

⊠ Explain two things that are wrong with the machine.

⊠ Finish the note and the letter correctly.

Writing a detailed description

Completing sentences

1 **Use the words to label the drawing.**

1 tail   **2** claws   **3** beak   **4** wing   **5** paws   **6** fur

a _____   b _____   c _____   d _____   e _____   f _____

2 **Use the picture to complete the text and the text to label the picture.**

The mantis prawn

Animals that kill other animals for their food are called predators. The mantis prawn is the fastest 1 _____ in the world.

2 _____ milliseconds (that's 1/200th of a second) after its claws get into a 3 _____ , the fish is dead. The one in the picture is 25 centimetres long but they can be 4 _____ centimetres long.

Some people eat them!

The mantis 5 _____ : The
6 _____ killer 7 _____ _____
world. Would you 8 _____ one for
dinner? This one is 25 centimetres
9 _____ but they can be
40 centimetres long. It has got
10 _____ that can kill a fish in five
milliseconds.

3 **Complete the sentences with words from exercise 1, above. Then guess the animal from the list below.**

1 This brightly coloured bird is one of the ones that can talk.

It has got a sharp _____ .

2 This animal is now the most popular pet in Britain. It has got

sharp little _____ .

3 This little, white animal is very good to eat! It has got a

small _____ .

| spider, cat, prawn, bear, lamb, parrot, shark, snake, frog |

Writing sentences

4 **Read the reports about four large predators. Eight sentences have mistakes. Re-write them correctly.**

The world's largest spider

The largest spider [1]of the world is the goliath tarantula. It is 25 centimetres from one leg to the other and it weighs 57 grams. It is called 'the bird-eating spider' but nobody knows why. It [2]eats usually frogs. It kills the frogs with the hairs on its legs.

As long as a bus – but more dangerous!

It can grow as [3]long a bus. It can swim at 24 kilometres per hour. And it can bite you in half with one bite. The shark in Steven Spielberg's film *Jaws* was a great white. But the largest shark is the whale shark. It can be twelve metres long. But sharks [4]doesn't usually eat people.

They need our help!

The brown bear is the second biggest bear in the world. The polar bear is [5]more big. But the brown bear is nearly two metres tall and weighs more than 468 kilos. It can kill with one of its huge [6]tails. But there are not many brown bears left in the world and they need our help.

A VERY LONG SNAKE

One kind of snake, the rock python, [7]can't be ten metres long. It kills by winding its body round and round the other animal until the other animal can't breathe. In some countries people [8]eats rock python. They say the eggs are very good!

5 **Work in pairs. Write five sentences describing five different animals, without saying what the animals are. Can your partner guess which five animals you are describing?**

Example: It has four paws, a long tail and sharp claws. (Answer: cat)

Putting sentences together

6 **Complete the sentences with *the one* or *the ones*.**

Example:
All spiders have eight legs. *The one* in the picture is the world's largest.
That bear is brown. *The ones* we saw at the zoo were black.

1 There are many different sharks. _____ in *Jaws* was a great white shark.

2 Bears need our help. _____ that need our help most are brown bears and polar bears.

3 Bears run faster than people think. _____ in the picture can run at 56 kilometres per hour.

4 All predators kill for food. _____ that kills fastest is the mantis prawn.

5 All snakes are predators. _____ that kill by winding their body round the other animal are called *constrictors*.

7 **Write a detailed description of an *imaginary* animal. Draw your animal and label the drawing.**

Here are some things to think about:

- Is it a killer?
- What does it eat?
- How long is it?
- How many paws has it got?
- What are its teeth like?
- Has it got a tail?
- Has it got wings?
- Can you eat it?
- · Can it eat you?
- Does it need our help?

Unit 3 At the tourist office

Writing dialogue

Completing sentences

1 **Write two lists. List 1 is places of interest for tourists in your country. List 2 is places of interest anywhere in the world.**

2 **Complete sentences 1–3 in the dialogue with the correct three of a–f.**

    a What is there   **c** What would you like   **e** Does that sound

    b Is that   **d** Where would you like   **f** What can we do

Mr Harrison and his daughter Melanie and son Peter are at the tourist office.

MR HARRISON:	Unfortunately, we have only two days here. 1_____ in that time?
TOURIST OFFICER:	What sort of things are you interested in?
MR HARRISON:	Well, I'm interested in the history of this country but I have my teenaged son and daughter here. (*He turns to Melanie and Peter.*) 2 _____ to do in our two days here?
MELANIE:	Not museums.
PETER:	Not art galleries.
MR HARRISON:	They think there's nothing for them to do here. That's not true is it?
TOURIST OFFICER:	I hope not! We have a very good market here. You can buy all sorts of interesting things. 3 _____ like fun?
PETER:	Yes! I'm looking for some trainers. Can you get trainers at the market?
TOURIST OFFICER:	I think so. And we also have a go-kart track here. (*to Melanie and Peter*) Do you like driving?
PETER:	No.
MELANIE:	Oh yes!

3 **Complete the sentences.**

    1 Peter is not interested in _____ but he likes _____.

    2 Melanie is not interested in _____ but she likes _____.

    3 If I were a tourist in my country I would _____

    _____.

Writing sentences

4 Read the dialogue. Write what the tourist officer says. Then read the dialogue aloud with a partner.

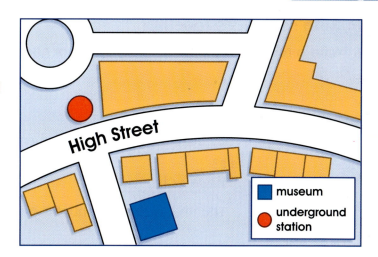

High Street

■ museum

● underground station

A dialogue in a tourist office

MAN: This map of your city is no good.

TOURIST OFFICER: **1** _____?

MAN: This is what's wrong with it: I went to High Street and there's no museum there. Look at the map. You see that symbol? That's the museum symbol, isn't it?

TOURIST OFFICER: **2** _____.

MAN: The underground symbol? You mean for underground train stations? Oh yes. I see now. It's a red circle. So what's the symbol for museums, then?

TOURIST OFFICER: **3** _____ .

MAN: *(looking at the map)* Blue square ... blue square .... But there aren't any blue squares on this map. Oh yes, there's one. Which museum is that?

TOURIST OFFICER: **4** _____ .

MAN: And what's in the Museum of the Moving Image?

TOURIST OFFICER: **5** _____

_____ .

MAN: Oh that sounds very good. I'm interested in cinema and TV. The early days, you say? And how photography started. That's very interesting. How do I get there?

5 Write three questions that a tourist might ask about three places of interest. You can use the lists you wrote at exercise 1 for ideas about places of interest. Ask a partner your three questions.

Putting sentences together

6 Write a reply to 1–5 with either *I think so* or *I hope not*.

Examples:

MELANIE: Does the market sell leather goods?

TOURIST OFFICER: I think so. _____

MR HARRISON: They think there's nothing for them to do here. That's not true is it?

TOURIST OFFICER: I hope not! _____

1 MR HARRISON: The underground symbol is a red circle, isn't it?

PETER: _____

2 MR HARRISON: Did we leave the map in the museum?

MRS HARRISON: _____ It's closed now.

3 MELANIE: Is Dad going to drive a go-kart?

PETER: _____ I want him to watch.

4 MELANIE: Do you want to come to the market with me?

PETER: _____ , but I don't know

if I'll have time.

5 PETER: Did the tourist officer give us only one map?

MELANIE: _____ We need three.

7 Work with a partner. Write a one-page dialogue at the tourist office. Then give your dialogue to another pair to read aloud while you listen. Here are some ideas but you can use your own ideas if you want to.

⋈ The tourist officer helps teenage tourists find things to do.

⋈ The tourist officer shows a tourist where things are on a map.

⋈ The tourist officer helps a family plan a two- or three-day visit to a city or area.

⋈ The tourist officer shows teenage tourists a leaflet about the area and explains it to them.

Writing notes, letters, posters and a website asking for and offering help

Completing sentences

1 **Write the words in the correct gap.**

ship beach rocks

Yesterday a **1** _____ hit some **2** _____ near South Beach, fifty miles from London. The ship was carrying oil. The oil is now on the sea and on the **3** _____ . It is an environmental disaster.

2 **Robert and David are talking about helping at South Beach. Complete the sentences.**

I'll ask Dad to take us to South Beach.

I'll ask Melanie **2** _____ _____ _____ _____ _____ .

Dad, can you **1** <u>take us to South Beach?</u>

Melanie, would you like to come to South Beach?

I'll e-mail friends and ask for help.

I'll **4** _____ _____ _____ about the environment from Mum.

Would you like **3** _____ _____ ?

Mum, can I borrow a book about the environment?

3 **Complete the sentences with offers of help.**

1 DAD: I'm free on Saturday, I'll <u>take you to</u> South Beach.

2 MELANIE: Yes, I'll _____ you to South Beach.

3 DAVID: I'll _____ and ask for help, too.

4 MUM: Yes, I'll let you _____ . And I'll help you search the World Wide Web for information, too.

Writing sentences

4 Write sentences offering help. Use the words and pictures below.

Robert and David wrote a letter to the people of South Beach offering help.

We'll help to ...
We'd like to ...
Can we help to ...
Would you like us to ...

get oil/beach

clean/birds

plant/trees

make/new beach

put detergent/oil

5 Write a poster to put up at school, asking people to help at the environmental disaster at South Beach. Write six or more sentences with these phrases:

Would you like to ...
Can you ...
Will you ...
Example: Would you like to help put detergent on the oil?

Putting sentences together

6 Write these sentences again with *as* and *so*.

Example:
We are interested in the environment. We can help with the environmental disaster.

As we are interested in the environment, we can help with the environmental disaster.

We are interested in the environment, so we can help with the environmental disaster.

1 We are good at science. We can test the sea for pollution.

2 We know about birds. We can help clean the oil off the birds.

3 My dad will take us to South Beach. We can help get oil off the beach.

7 Work on your own. Write a note to a friend offering help with an environmental disaster.

8 Work in small groups. Write and design a website* asking for help with an environmental disaster (oil on the beach or something else). You can design the website on paper or on a computer.

✄ Describe the drawings as well as writing the words. For example 'This is a drawing of people on the beach. They are making a new beach.'

✄ Use your work on exercise 5 to help you.

✄ Say who people must contact if they want to help. How should they contact this person? At home? At school?

*A website is like a poster that you can see on the Internet.

Unit 5 Don't worry but …

Writing notes explaining emergency situations

Completing sentences

1 **With a partner, say what you would do in these emergency situations. Then write another emergency situation.**

- ⋈ Your key breaks in the lock. You can't get in.
- ⋈ A pipe bursts in the bathroom.
- ⋈ Your little brother is ill at school.
- ⋈ The ceiling falls down.
- ⋈ The cooker catches fire.
- ⋈ A neighbour is shouting for help.
- ⋈ _____

2 **Complete the sentences.**

At 1:00, Melanie wrote this note. ▶

At 1:30, Melanie learned that Peter had cut his leg. The school knew what to do. Melanie has gone to the hospital with him. She'll phone from the hospital.

> Peter's school have just phoned. Peter's ill, I think. I've gone to get him. Don't worry! – Melanie

At 1:40, Melanie wrote this note. ▶

> Peter's school 1 _____ earlier today. Peter's leg is 2 _____ but they 3 _____ _____ at his school. I'm on my way with
> 4 _____ _____ _____ Peter. I'll 5 _____ you
> 6 _____ there. Don't worry! – Melanie

3 **Complete the sentences about emergency situations.**

1 When I saw all the water in the bathroom I _____

_____ .

2 There was a fire in the kitchen but I knew what to do. I _____

_____ .

3 Nobody knew what to give our neighbour when she was ill, so _____

_____ .

Writing sentences

4 **Write the captions and the speech bubbles in full in the correct places.**

captions:
a But/knew/what/do
b Part of/ceiling fell down
c /made holes in/ceiling and/ water/ran out
d /crack appeared/in ceiling/ in kitchen

speech bubbles:
e We need/make/small holes/ceiling
f Watch out!/It/coming down!
g Oh no! There's/crack/ceiling
h There/burst pipe./I know/do.

Laura and Melanie see a crack in the kitchen ceiling.

5 **Work with a partner. Write the story of an emergency in one sentence. Who, in the class, can write the longest correct sentence?**

Writing Tip

Join parts of a sentence with *and, but* and *so*.

Putting sentences together

6 Write *what* or *when* in these sentences.

1 _____ I saw our neighbour on the floor I called an ambulance.

2 I knew _____ to do when the water pipe burst, so don't worry.

3 I went with her to hospital _____ the ambulance came.

4 We don't know _____ to do, so we've gone to get help.

5 _____ the cooker caught fire I called the fire brigade.

7 Write notes explaining these emergency situations.

1 The cooker has caught fire.

2 There is a car crash outside.

3 A neighbour is locked in her flat.

4 Another situation. You can use the one you wrote in exercise 1, if you want to.

Writing biography and autobiography

Completing sentences

1 Write your birth date and the name of the town where you were born. Tell a partner when and where you were born, about your family and your early life.

_____

2 Look at the information about Orville Wright and complete the sentences.

> **Name:** Orville Wright
> **Born:** In 1871 at Dayton, Ohio, USA
> **Died:** In 1948
> **Famous for:** With his brother Wilbur, the first ever powered flight
> **When:** On December 17, 1903
> **Where:** At Kitty Hawk, North Carolina, USA
> **How long:** For fifty-nine seconds
> **How far:** 260 metres

Orville Wright 1 _____ born 2 _____ 1871 3 _____ Dayton, Ohio, USA. Orville and his brother Wilbur are famous 4 _____ the first ever powered 5 _____ in their aeroplane _Flyer 1_. Cars were new in the 1900s and Wilbur and Orville Wright put a car engine in their aeroplane. Orville was the pilot 6 _____ December 17, 1903 7 _____ Kitty Hawk, North Carolina, while his brother watched him. The first time the aeroplane was in the air for only twelve seconds, flying at three metres above the ground! But later that day Orville flew 8 _____ fifty-nine seconds. He flew 260 9 _____ . By 1905 they flew 36 kilometres and they flew until 1912 when Wilbur died.

3 **Complete the sentences and guess who the people are.**

1 He _____ born _____ 1942 and he was known as 'the Greatest'. He was a boxer and he is a Muslim.

2 He was born in 1940. He came from a poor family in Brazil. His _____ is Edson Arantes do Nascimento but he has another name that is better known. He is famous _____ being the best footballer of all time.

Writing sentences

4 **Read the biography then answer the questions. Write full sentences.**

MUHAMMAD ALI

① *1960 Olympics: gold medal in boxing*

② *World heavyweight boxing champion!*

③ *The best known face in the world*

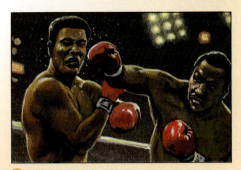

④ *1971: lost to Joe Frazier*

1 What did Muhammad Ali do in 1960?

In 1960, Muhammad Ali won an Olympic gold medal in boxing.

2 What did Muhammad Ali do next?

3 What did people say about Muhammad Ali's face?

4 What happened in 1971?

5 **Work with a partner or on your own. Write five sentences of biography about five different men and women. They can be famous men and women or your friends and family. Can a partner guess who the people are?**

Putting sentences together

6 Write these sentences again with *while* or *until*.

Examples:
Muhammad Ali had the best known face in the world. He was world heavyweight boxing champion.

Muhammad Ali had the best known face in the world <u>while</u> he was world heavyweight boxing champion.

Muhammad Ali was called Cassius Clay. He became a Muslim.

Muhammad Ali was called Cassius Clay <u>until</u> he became a Muslim.

1 I learned to play the guitar. I was living in Manchester.
2 Pelé was the greatest footballer in the world. He stopped playing in 1978.
3 Muhammad Ali really was 'the Greatest'. He was the heavyweight champion of the world.
4 The two Wright brothers were pilots. Wilbur died in 1912.
5 I lived in Edinburgh. My family moved to London in 1999.

7 Write an autobiography and a biography.
Write a paragraph of autobiography (the story of your own life).
Write about:

- when and where you were born.
- how many brothers and sisters you have got.
- your early life and your time at school.

8 At home, write a biography. First you need to find the information, then write a paragraph about someone you are interested in. Write about:

- when and where the person was born.
- the person's family.
- the person's early life.
- the person's life now. Why are you interested in him or her?

Writing personal anecdotes

Completing sentences

1 **Work with a partner or on your own. Here are three situations. In your exercise book write a sentence about what you did next in each situation.**

  1 You started to wash in the morning and there was no water.
  2 On your way to school a lost child asked you for help.
  3 When you got to school it was locked and there was nobody there.

2 **Complete the sentences using the picture story.**

Paul and Robert were walking to school.

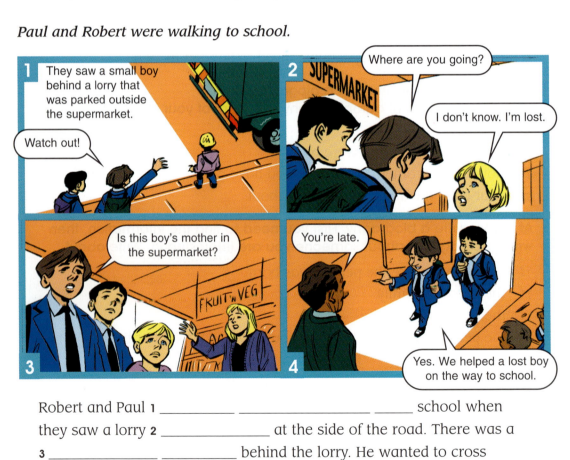

Robert and Paul 1 _____ _____ _____ school when
they saw a lorry 2 _____ at the side of the road. There was a
3 _____ _____ behind the lorry. He wanted to cross
4 _____ _____ but Paul 5 _____ 'Watch out!'
The little boy was 6 _____ . Paul and Robert took the boy
7 _____ _____ _____ . They were looking for

8 _____ _____ _____ . In the supermarket a woman ran to Paul and Robert. She was the boy's mother. Paul and Robert were late for school because of the **9** _____ _____ outside the supermarket but when they told their teacher the story he wasn't angry.

3 Complete the sentences. Use your imagination.

1 When I got home from school I found that I had Laura's bag so _____

_____.

2 I've just won a competition! I had to _____

_____.

3 Last week we all went for a picnic and _____

_____.

Writing sentences

4 Write *three* of these sentences in the correct place in the anecdote.

a There was a child outside the supermarket.

b Something really great happened to me last week.

c We're all going to New York!

d I also had to do a drawing.

1 _____

_____ I won a competition! I had to write a sentence about Tesbury's supermarket. I wrote 'The food sold at Tesbury's is better than the food sold on the Moon.'

2 _____

_____ I did a drawing of a Moon man eating Tesbury's Cornflakes. The Moon man was green, had three arms, one eye and long blue hair. I've won a holiday for the family!

3 _____

_____

5 Write the next sentence of two anecdotes. Use your imagination.

1 Something really great happened to me the other day.

_____

_____

2 Something funny happened to me the other day.

_____

_____

6 Now read your sentences to a partner. With your partner, write one more sentence for each anecdote.

Putting sentences together

7 Write the sentences again like the example.

Example:
The boy was behind a lorry. The lorry was *parked* at the side of the road.

The boy was behind a lorry <u>parked</u> at the side of the road.

1 I like the chocolate. The chocolate is *sold* at Tesbury's.

2 That's the bag. The bag was *taken* by Laura.

3 I like all subjects. The subjects are *taught* at this school.

4 This is the hospital. It was *opened* last year.

5 Here are some photos of my holiday in New York. I *won* the holiday in a competition.

8 Write a personal anecdote. Start with either *Something really great happened to me the other day* or *Something funny happened to me the other day*. Write a paragraph.

Composition 3: Teacher's notes and answers

Composition 3 is the third of the three-book series. Continuing from *Composition 1* and *2*, it develops writing skills for 13–15-year-old elementary–intermediate pupils.

The characters

All the boys and girls from books 1 and 2 are also in book 3. They do things that are fun to learn about – like going to a go-kart track.

The structure of the book

As with books 1 and 2, all the units in *Composition 3* have this structure:
Page 1: Completing sentences
Page 2: Writing sentences
Page 3: Putting sentences together

The structure of each unit

Section 1 – Completing sentences

What the pupils write on page 1 is used again on pages 2 and 3.

Task 1
This task gets the pupils thinking about the subject of the unit and it starts them writing single words or lists. Pupils often tell a partner what they have written, so learning to write is supported by speaking.

Task 2
In task 2, typically, pupils are shown two different pieces of communication. In unit 1 these are a note and a formal letter. Both pieces of communication are gapped and the gaps from one can be written in by reading and understanding the other.

Task 3: Complete the sentences
In task 3, pupils complete sentences using information from task 2. These sentence completions help with the tasks coming next, usually with task 6. In unit 1 pupils are helped with the links *whenever* and *as soon as* which they practise in task 6. Item 2 in task 3 actually models *whenever* for the pupils.

Section 2 – Writing sentences

What pupils write on page 2 is used again on page 3

Task 4
There is a variety of exercise types at task 4 but all of them involve pupils writing complete sentences in a given context. For example in unit 1 pupils have a choice of sentences and they have to write the correct one into the correct speech bubble.

Task 5: Write sentences
This is the sentence-level free stage: Pupils write sentences of their own about the theme of the unit. In unit 1 the sentences are about technology going wrong.

Section 3 – Putting sentences together

Task 6
Task 6 helps pupils to join two sentences in two different ways. The ways of joining sentences have been introduced earlier in the unit and so has all the vocabulary in this task.

Task 7: Write a paragraph
Task 7 is the culmination of the unit. Pupils write a paragraph, a leaflet, a website, a booklet, a dialogue or a note, depending on the theme of the unit. Guidance is given that refers pupils back to their earlier work in the unit, but in some units they are also invited to write a little more, unguided.

Answer key

Unit 1

1 1c 2b 3a
2 1 are two   2 paper keeps jamming
  3 time I put paper in the printer it jams
  4 the printer's always printing out badly
  5 print comes out too black
3 open answers
4 1 I'm phoning the mobile phone firm.
  2 What's wrong with your phone?
  3 I can't hear anyone!
  4 But I've never talked to anybody!
5 1 Mario is always in the same room of the castle.
  2 The wheel is always coming off.
    The saddle keeps falling off.
  3 The headphones don't work.
    It keeps playing slowly.
6 1 *Whenever/As soon as* I press 'Save', the computer loses the file.
  2 *Whenever/As soon as* I move the mouse, the computer loses the words on the screen.
  3 *Whenever/As soon as* I switch on the TV, the picture goes black and white.
  4 *Whenever/As soon as* I change channels on the TV, I lose the sound.
7 **and 8** open answers

Unit 2

1 a4 b6 c2 d1 e5 f3
2 1 killer 2 Five 3 fish 4 40 5 prawn
  6 fastest 7 in the 8 eat 9 long 10 claws

3 1 beak – parrot   2 claws – cat
  3 tail – lamb
4 1 The largest spider in the world is the
     goliath tarantula.
  2 It usually eats frogs.
  3 It can grow as long as a bus.
  4 But sharks don't usually eat people.
  5 The polar bear is bigger.
  6 It can kill with one of its huge paws.
  7 One kind of snake, the rock python, can
     be ten metres long.
  8 In some countries people eat rock python.
5 open answers
6 1 The one   2 The ones   3 The one
  4 The one   5 The ones
7 open answers

Unit 3

1 open answers
2 1f   2c   3e
3 1 art galleries   shopping
  2 museums   go-karts
  3 open answer
4 suggested answers:
  1 What's wrong with it?
  2 No, it's the underground symbol.
  3 A blue square.
  4 Museum of the Moving Image.
  5 The early days of television and cinema
     and how photography started.
5 open answers
6 1 I think so.   2 I hope not.   3 I hope not.
  4 I think so.   5 I hope not.
7 open answers

Unit 4

1 1 ship   2 rocks   3 beach
2 2 to come to South Beach
  3 to help
  4 borrow a book
3 2 Yes, I'll go with you to South Beach
  3 I'll e-mail friends and ask for help, too.
  4 Yes, I'll let you borrow a book.
4 example answers:
  1 We'll help to get oil off the beach.
  2 Can we help to clean the birds?
  3 Can we help to plant trees?
  4 Can we help to make a new beach?
  5 We'd like to put detergent on the oil.
5 example answers:
  1 Would you like to get oil off the beach?
  2 Can you clean the birds?
  3 Would you like to plant trees?
  4 Can you make a new beach?
  5 Will you put detergent on the oil?
6 1 As we are good at science, we can test the
     sea for pollution. / We are good at science,
     so we can test the sea for pollution.

2 As we know about birds, we can help
  clean the oil off the birds. / We know
  about birds, so we can help clean the oil
  off the birds.
3 As my dad will take us to South Beach, we
  can help get oil off the beach. / My dad
  will take us to South Beach, so we can
  help get oil off the beach.
7 open answers
8 open answers

Unit 5

1 open answers
2 1 phoned   2 cut   3 knew what to do
  4 to the hospital   5 phone   6 from
3 open answers
4 1 Oh no! There's a crack in the ceiling!
  2 A crack appeared in the ceiling in the
     kitchen.
  3 Watch out! It's coming down!
  4 Part of the ceiling fell down.
  5 There's a burst pipe.
     I know what to do.
  6 But I knew what to do.
  7 We need to make small holes in the
     ceiling.
  8 We made holes in the ceiling and the
     water ran out.
5 open answers
6 1 When   2 what   3 when   4 what   5 When
7 open answers

Unit 6

1 open answers
2 1 was   2 in   3 at   4 for   5 flight   6 on
  7 at   8 for   9 metres
3 1 was, in (Muhammad Ali)   2 name, for
  (Pelé)
4 2 Then he became world heavyweight
     boxing champion.
  3 People said he had the best known face in
     the world.
  4 He lost a boxing match for the first time
     to Joe Frazier.
5 open answers
6 1 I learned to play the guitar while I was
     living in Manchester.
  2 Pelé was the greatest footballer in the
     world until he stopped playing in 1978.
  3 Muhammad Ali really was 'the Greatest'
     while he was the heavyweight champion
     of the world.
  4 The two Wright brothers were pilots until
     Wilbur died in 1912.
  5 I lived in Edinburgh until my family
     moved to London in 1999.
7 open answers
8 open answers

Unit 7

1 open answers
2 1 were walking to   2 parked
   3 little boy/small boy   4 the road
   5 shouted   6 lost   7 into the supermarket
   8 the boy's mother   9 lost boy
3 open answers
4 1b   2d   3c
5 open answers
6 open answers
7 1 I like the chocolate *sold* at Tesbury's.
   2 That's the bag *taken* by Laura.
   3 I like all subjects *taught* at this school.
   4 This is the hospital *opened* last year.
   5 Here are some photos of my holiday in
      New York I *won* in a competition.
8 open answers

Unit 8

1 open answers
2 1e   2g   3c   4d   5f   6a   7b
3 open answers
4 suggested answers:
   2 So at five to twelve she ran home.
   3 The prince found the shoe.
   4 I want to marry her.
   5 The sisters tried it on.
   6 Cinderella married the prince.
5 open answers
6 1 He was walking along the street but
      suddenly he started running.
   2 They didn't know what to do but next day
      they found out.
   3 I was playing football with my friends
      when suddenly I saw a monster.
   4 It was a nice day so my friends and I went
      for a picnic in the desert.
   5 A long time ago there was a very poor
      man who lived in a tiny village.
7 open answers

Unit 9

1 open answers
2 1 an adventure film   2 the British actress
   3 the American film star   4 The story of the
   5 were very good   6 showed   7 everybody
   8 there was   9 played by   10 were a bit
   boring
3 open answers
4 suggested answers:
   2 He looked at the paper of a boy sitting
      near him.
   3 The boy said 'Don't copy!'
   4 Eric copied the wrong exam.
5 1 I like the film because Tom, played by
      John Smith, is such a clever character.
   2 The special effects were clever. You
      couldn't see it was a model and the ship
      looked real.

3 The audience were interested because it
   was as if the film was finished quickly.
4 The film is good for audiences in this
   country. We like that kind of film.
6 1 But X is the funniest character I've seen.
   2 But X is the best film I've seen.
   3 But X is the worst film I've seen.
   4 But the special effects in X were the most
      real I've seen.
   5 But the acting in X was the best I've seen.
7 open answers

Unit 10

1 open answers
2 1 good news   2 in   3 America   4 present
   5 Laura's   6 best moment of the day
   7 anything he wants   8 happy   9 sad
3 open answers
4 1 Why didn't he come?
   2 (It makes me angry) when friends keep
      asking for help with their homework.
   3 I think it's awful when people talk during
      a film.
   4 I hate standing in a queue.
   5 Can you lend me some money?
5 possible ways of starting the sentences
   1 It makes me angry when …
   2 X makes me angry.
   3 I don't like it when …
   4 I hate it when …
   5 I think it's awful when …
   6 People shouldn't …
6 1 It makes me angry when people always
      ask for help with their homework.
   2 I love to get a letter in the post.
   3 I really enjoy going to the cinema.
   4 It makes me furious when the bus is late.
   5 Simon doesn't like standing in a queue.
7 open answers

Unit 11

1 pedal, track, crash helmet, race suit, brake
2 1 £70   2 race suit   3 crash helmet
   4 equipment   5 to drive   6 the accelerator
   7 restaurant   8 watch the karts   9 Birthday
   10 cake
3 1 you get a race suit, gloves and a crash
      helmet
   2 you can drive a go-kart
   3 you can eat at the restaurant
4 1 She saw an advertisement.
   2 They all had a good time.
   3 After showing us the equipment, the
      instructor gave us a safety briefing.
   4 She drove much faster than I did!
   5 She drove so fast, much faster than
   6 But the cake was as good as mine.
   7 After driving round for an hour we had a
      lovely party.

8 I didn't know that boys from my class
  were coming.
  B Melanie   C Laura's mum   D Laura
5 1 Melanie drove much more slowly than
    I did.
  2 Laura's mum and dad watched us from
    the restaurant while we were driving.
  3 I usually make Laura's birthday cake
    myself but having the cake at the
    restaurant after watching the girls on the
    track was my idea.
6 1 Before driving the go-karts on the track,
    they got a safety briefing.
  2 After having fun on the track for an hour,
    they went to the restaurant.
  3 After visiting the go-kart track, Melanie
    went with Laura to the party.
  4 Before going out on the track, Melanie and
    Laura put their crash helmets on.
  5 Before putting her crash helmet on, Laura
    put her race suit on.
7 open answers

Unit 12

1 open answers
2 1a   2a   3b   4b   5b   6a   7b   8a   9b
  10b   11a   12a   13a
3 open answers
4 2 He was born in London.
  3 His address is 137 Rutland Street, London.
  4 He goes to Queen Mary School, London.
  5 He is in year 11.
  6 His hobbies are swimming, lifesaving,
    table tennis and football.
  7 He has been learning French since 1999
    and German since 2000.
  8 He can use a computer (and knows/with)
    Word 7 and DOS. He can do lifesaving.
  9 He has a Swimming Coaching Certificate
    (with Lifesaving) and an IT Certificate. He
    is taking ten GCSEs this summer.
  10 He has been working in his father's shoe
    shop every summer since 2000.
5 open answers
6 1 I have been using Word 7 at home and at
    school since 2000.
  2 I was born in 1989.
  3 I have been learning English since 1999.
  4 I have been helping in my father's shop
    since 2000.
  5 I have been coaching young swimmers
    since 1998.
7 open answers

Unit 13

1 open answers
2 1c   2e   3h   4g   5b   6f   7d   8a
3 open answers

4 example answers:
  2 I would like to see fewer old films on TV
    because they are very boring and the
    people all talk too much.
  3 It seems to me that there is too much
    football on TV. Not everybody is
    interested in sport but I enjoy watching
    our team on TV.
  4 My favourite programme on TV is called
    'Film Night'. I never go to sleep while it's
    on because it's very exciting and I think
    there should be more programmes like it
    on TV.
  5 It seems to me that the best drama series
    on TV is 'Hospital' because the stories are
    very exciting, the acting is excellent and
    you always want to know what happens
    because it's so interesting.
5 example answers:
  2 In my opinion my favourite team isn't on
    often enough but they show some good
    foreign teams.
  3 It seems to me that it keeps me up to date
    about what is going on in my country.
  4 I think it makes me laugh because the
    people do silly things.
6 1 I think the news is the best programme
    on TV at the moment.
  2 It seems to me that this is an excellent
    drama series with good acting.
  3 There should be programmes made
    specially for teenagers.
  4 There should be more programmes like
    this.
  5 I would like to see more really excellent
    sports programmes.
7 open answers

Unit 14

1 open answers
2 open answers
3 open answers
4 2 Robert wants to work as a doctor.
  3 Robert might work as an engineer.
  4 Robert wants to help Moon people.
  5 Robert might live on Earth.
  6 Robert might commute to the Moon.
5 open answers
6 1 I hope to be rich and happy in a few
    years' time.
  2 I hope to stay in this country when I have
    my own family.
  3 I hope to go on holiday in a few months'
    time.
  4 I hope to get a car when I'm old enough.
  5 I hope to get a car in a few years' time.
7 open answers

Unit 8 Stories we all know

Writing narrative

Completing sentences

1 **Write the titles of two stories that everybody in your country knows. Then write key words (the most important words) for each of them. Use a dictionary.**

   Example: Story: Cinderella   Key words: sisters, party, midnight

   1 _____

   2 _____

2 **Here is the start of a story. Write sentences a–g in the correct places.**

   a Then she went
   b at five minutes to midnight
   c One day, the older sisters
   d Suddenly, a fairy appeared

   e A very poor girl lived
   f was a lovely dress
   g like a servant

Cinderella

1 _____ with her two older sisters. The girl, Cinderella, did all the housework. She was **2** _____ to her older sisters. **3** _____ were going to a big party given by the king. Cinderella couldn't go. She had no clothes to wear. **4** _____ in the room. 'Cinderella, you can go to the party,' said the fairy. 'But you must be back by midnight.' And there, in Cinderella's room **5** _____ . Cinderella put it on. **6** _____ outside . There was a coach and four beautiful horses, waiting for her. So Cinderella went to the party. But **7** _____ she didn't want to leave.

3 **Work with a partner. Complete the sentences in any way you like.**

   1 They were having a picnic when suddenly _____ .

   2 I saw a monster and then _____ .

   3 A man gave me some money. Next day _____ .

Writing sentences

4 **Here is the end of the story of Cinderella. Write one more sentence for each picture, using the words given.**

Cinderella enjoyed the party.

She talked to the prince.
talked

She had to leave at midnight.

_____

ran

She ran so fast she dropped her shoe.

_____

found

The prince said, 'Find the girl who wore the shoe.'

_____

want/marry

Next day, soldiers came to Cinderella's house with the shoe.

_____

tried on

The shoe was too small for her sisters, but it fitted Cinderella.

_____

marry

5 **Write the first sentences of the two stories you named in exercise 1.**

Putting sentences together

6 Write the two sentences again as one sentence. Use the correct connecting word.

Example:
I turned round. He was gone. (but/while)

I turned round but he was gone.

1 He was walking along the street. He started running.
   (so/but suddenly)

2 They didn't know what to do. They found out.
   (but next day/and one day)

3 I was playing football with my friends. I saw a monster.
   (when suddenly/while suddenly)

4 It was a nice day. My friends and I went for a picnic in the desert.
   (but/so)

5 A long time ago there was a very poor man. He lived in a tiny village.
   (which/who)

Writing Tip

When you write a story, start with key words. Then write sentences from the key words. Then put the sentences together. (See exercise 1, exercise 5 and exercise 7)

7 Work with a partner or on your own. Write one of the stories you started in exercises 1 and 5. Write a paragraph.

The best film I've ever seen

Writing a review

Completing sentences

1 Write the names of your favourite films and favourite film stars. Has your partner got the same ones as you?

_____

_____

2 Write the correct choices to complete the film review.

My favourite film is called 'Titanic'. It's

1 _____ .

    was an adventure film/an adventure film

The stars are **2** _____

    the British actress/the Britain actress

Kate Winslet and **3** _____

    the America film star/the American film star

Leonardo DiCaprio. **4** _____

    The story of the/A story of the

'Titanic' is true. In 1912 the 'Titanic' was the most modern ship in the world. Nobody thought it could go down. But it did. It sank in the Atlantic Ocean and 1,405 people died. It was one of the most exciting films I have seen and the special effects **5** _____ . Some of the film

    was very good/were very good

6 _____ the real 'Titanic', four kilometres under the sea. When water came

    showed/was shown

into the ship in the film, **7** _____ in the audience felt as if they were really on the ship.

    anybody/everybody

In the film **8** _____ a girl called Rose, **9** _____ Kate Winslet.

    it was/there was   played by/the actress was

When the ship went down she was saved by an American boy called Jack, played by Leonardo DiCaprio, but Jack died. I thought the scenes with Rose and Jack **10** _____ .

    was a bit boring/were a bit boring

3 Complete the sentences.

1 The best film or TV programme I have ever seen (or the best book I have ever read) is _____ .

2 I like my favourite film (or book or TV programme) because _____

_____ .

3 This film (or TV programme or book) is about _____

_____ .

4 I didn't like this film (or book or TV programme) because _____

_____ .

Writing sentences

4 Write what happened in each scene of the video.

The comic character Eric Snell, played by Sam Riley, is one of the funniest comic characters ever.

1 Eric took an exam.
   take

2 _____
   look

3 _____
   say

4 _____
   copy

5 Write sentences disagreeing with these sentences.

Example:
I think it was one of the funniest, best acted films I've ever seen.

I think it was one of the silliest, most badly acted films I've ever seen.

1 I don't like the film because Tom, played by John Smith, is such a silly character.

2 The special effects were stupid. You could see it was a model and the ship didn't look real.

3 The audience were bored because it felt as if the film was taking hours.

4 The film is not for audiences in this country. We don't like that kind of film.

Putting sentences together

6 Write a second sentence using a superlative, like the example.

Example:
'Titanic' is <u>exciting</u>. But 'Jaws' is <u>the most exciting</u> film I've seen.

1 Eric Snell is a funny character.

2 'Toy Story' was a good film.

3 I think 'Oliver Twist' was a bad film.

4 The special effects in 'Titanic' were quite real.

5 The acting in 'Shakespeare in Love' was good.

7 Write a review of a film, a TV programme or a book.
Write about:

- what the film is called, what type of film it is (adventure, comedy) and who the stars are.
- what happens in the film.
- the special effects and how the film is filmed. (Do the scenes look beautiful?)
- how the audience felt about the film.
- your opinion and how the film compares with other films.

Unit 10 I was happy./I was furious.

Writing about emotions

Completing sentences

1 **Which small things in your daily life make you happy? Use a dictionary. Has your partner got the same list?**

Example: *finishing my homework*

_____

_____

2 **Work with a partner. Use the speech bubbles to complete the captions and the captions to complete the speech bubbles.**

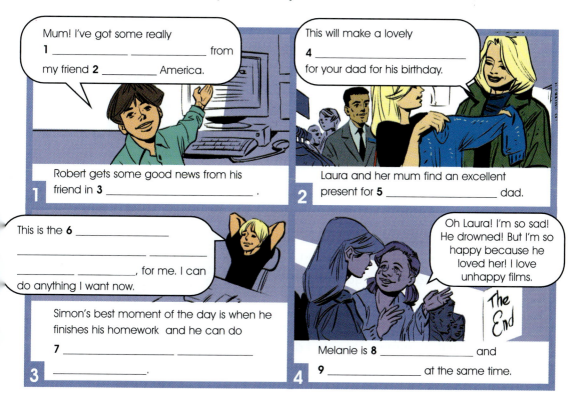

3 **Complete the sentences about what makes you happy in your daily life.**

1 My favourite moment of the day is _____ .

2 What makes me happy is when _____ .

3 I think it's great that _____ .

Writing sentences

4 Read the dialogue. Write what Robert says. Then read the dialogue aloud with a partner.

SIMON: Paul didn't come to the football match yesterday. He *said* he was coming. I hate it when people do that.

ROBERT: 1 _____?

SIMON: I don't know. He didn't give me a reason. It makes me so furious. What makes you angry?

ROBERT: 2 _____
_____ .

SIMON: Yes, I agree! It's OK to help friends with their homework sometimes, but they shouldn't keep asking for help. Are you coming to the cinema this evening?

ROBERT: 3 No, _____
_____ .

SIMON: Well, I think it's awful when people talk during the film too, but you can still come, can't you?

ROBERT: 4 _____ .

SIMON: What do you mean, you hate standing in a queue? We'll go early. We can go in without standing in a queue then.

ROBERT: 5 _____?

SIMON: No, I can't! I've got enough money for myself but no money for you. I don't like it when people want me to lend them money all the time.

5 Write six sentences about what makes you angry in your daily life. All six must start in a different way.

Putting sentences together

6 Change the sentences but keep the same meaning using the words in brackets.

Example:
People who leave before the end of a film make me angry. (awful)
I think it's awful when people leave before the end of a film.

1 I hate people who always ask for help with their homework. (angry)
2 It's great to get a letter in the post. (love)
3 I love going to the cinema. (really enjoy)
4 I don't like it when the bus is late. (furious)
5 Simon hates standing in a queue. (like)

7 Imagine that all the small things that make you angry or all the small things that make you happy in daily life happened in one day. Write a letter or e-mail to a friend about that day.

⋈ Introduce the day as a very bad one or as a very good one.
⋈ Say what happened and how you felt about each thing that makes you angry or happy.

Writing a detailed description of an event

Completing sentences

1 **Tick the words that have something to do with go-karts. Write some more words. Use a dictionary.**

pedal   track   mouse   crash helmet   window   race suit   brake

_____

2 **Work with a partner. Read the advertisement for go-karting and complete the picture story.**

KARTING AT ITS BEST!

Before you start your fun drive on a go-kart we supply you with a race suit, gloves and a crash helmet. After giving you this equipment we give you a safety briefing and instructions on how to drive the karts. Karts are very easy to control with just two pedals, a brake for STOP and an accelerator for GO. After having fun with the karts you can eat at our beautiful track-side restaurant. You can watch the karts from the restaurant! AND you can have a birthday party at our restaurant, complete with birthday cake. Call 01206 799511 for details.

5 minutes	£6
10 minutes	£10
20 minutes	£16
60 minutes	£35

Laura's surprise birthday party

1 Two children for one hour. That's **1** _____ .

2 **2** _____ **3** _____

3 I'm going to give you your **4** _____ and tell you how **5** _____ .

4 the brake **6** _____

5 This is a lovely **7** _____ . We can **8** _____ _____ from here.

6 Happy **9** _____ , Laura. Here's your **10** _____ .

3 **Complete the sentences in your notebook.**

   1 Before driving a go-kart at a go-kart track …

   2 After listening to a safety briefing …

   3 After having fun on the go-kart track …

Writing sentences

4 **Use the words to write sentences. Then write the name of the person speaking: Laura, Melanie, Laura's mum or Laura's dad.**

A Laura's dad

My wife had the idea of a surprise birthday party for my daughter.
1 _____ Laura and a friend could go to a go-kart
                          she/see/advertisement
track. After driving round for an hour they could have a surprise party. It was very expensive. But a lot
of Laura's friends came to the party. Melanie and her little brother came. And Robert, Paul and
Simon from her class. **2** _____
                                        they all/have/good time

B _____

3 _____
              After/show/equipment, instructor/give/safety briefing
And then we just drove! The karts were very easy to control. It's best if you don't brake too much
in a go-kart. Laura was really good at it.
4 _____
              she/drive/much faster/I did!

C _____

We could see the track very well from the restaurant. Bill and I had a very nice meal and
watched Laura. I was a bit worried at first.
5 _____ Melanie!
              she/drive/so fast, much faster
And I was pleased that the surprise birthday cake was so good. I usually make Laura's
birthday cake myself. **6** _____
                                        but/cake/good as/mine

D _____

Mum and Dad gave me a lovely birthday. My race suit was red which looked good with my hair.
And the gloves and helmet were quite comfortable.
7 _____
              after/drive round for/hour/have/lovely party
8 _____
              I/not know that/boys from/class/come
They all sang 'Happy Birthday!' It was great.

5 Write these sentences again from the point of view of the person in brackets.

Example: LAURA: Mum and Dad gave me a lovely birthday. (Laura's dad)

> Laura's dad: My wife and I gave Laura a lovely birthday.

1 MELANIE: Laura drove much faster than I did. (Laura)

2 LAURA'S MUM: Bill and I watched the girls from the restaurant, while they were driving. (Melanie)

3 LAURA'S DAD: My wife usually makes Laura's birthday cake herself but having the cake at the restaurant after watching the girls on the track was her idea. (Laura's mum)

Putting sentences together

6 Write the two sentences again as one sentence with *before* or *after* + *-ing*

Example: They had a good time at the party. Laura and her family went home.(after)

> After having a good time at the party, Laura and her family went home.

1 They drove go-karts on the track. They got a safety briefing. (before)

2 They had fun on the track for an hour. They went to the restaurant. (after)

3 She visited the go-kart track. Melanie went with Laura to the party. (after)

4 They went out on the track. Melanie and Laura put their crash helmets on. (before)

5 She put on her crash helmet. Laura put her race suit on. (before)

7 Write about 1 or 2 below.

1 Write a detailed description of a visit to a go-kart track. Write from the point of view of Laura *or* Melanie *or* Laura's mum *or* Laura's dad. You can use the names of your own family and friends if you want to. After writing your description, read descriptions written from another point of view.

Example first sentences:

LAURA: My mum saw an advertisement for a birthday party at a go-kart track.

MELANIE: My friend Laura's mum saw an advertisement for a ... .

LAURA'S DAD: My wife saw an advertisement for ... .

LAURA'S MUM: I saw an advertisement for ... .

2 Write about a nice day out that you have had. Perhaps a picnic or a birthday party or a visit to a big football match – anything at all!

Unit 12 My life

Writing a CV and an application for a holiday job

Completing sentences

1 Write three or four things that you can do and that you are interested in.

Examples: speak English, swim, use computers

_____

2 Read Robert's letter of application for a holiday job. Write the formal English each time. The other one is correct but informal.

1 _____ ,
       a Dear Sir or Madam **b** Hello

2 _____ in today's *Daily News* for
    a I am replying to your advertisement **b** I saw your advert

3 _____ at the new Holiday Centre for
     a someone who can teach kids to swim **b** a swimming instructor

teenagers. **4** _____ instructing the fifteen-year-olds.
       a I want the job of **b** I am applying for the job of

5 _____ a fifteen-year-old instructor for the
    a You said in the advert that you wanted **b** You advertised for

fifteen-year-olds and I am fifteen. **6** _____ I **7** _____
              a At the moment **b** Right now   **a** go to **b** am a pupil at

Bryant Road School. I am in year 11. **8** _____
                       a Among my qualifications is **b** One thing I have got is

a Swimming Coaching Certificate (with Lifesaving). I am an excellent swimmer!
9 _____ 13 July, which is the start of our school summer
    a I can come and teach **b** I am available from

holidays until 25 August, when my family are going on holiday.
10 _____
     a I can come and see you, if you like. **b** I would be happy to come for interview if selected.

11 _____
    a I enclose a CV. **b** Here's some information about me.

12 _____
    a Yours faithfully, **b** See you soon, then,

13 _____
    a Robert Simpson **b** Bob

3 Complete the sentences.

1 I am very good at _____ at school.

2 I have been learning English _____ .

3 My summer holidays from school this year are from _____ to _____ .

Writing sentences

4 Look at Robert's CV and write complete sentences from it.

CV: Robert Simpson
Born: 1989, London
Address: 137 Rutland Street, London, tel: 020-7563-5192
School: Queen Mary School, London
Year: 11
Hobbies: swimming, lifesaving, table tennis, football
Languages: French – (since 1999), German – (since 2000)
Skills: computer – (5 years) Word 7 and DOS, lifesaving
Qualifications: Swimming Coaching Certificate (with Lifesaving), IT (Information Technology) Certificate, taking ten GCSEs this summer
Work experience: have worked in my father's shoe shop every summer since 2000

1 Born when? <u>He was born in 1989.</u>

2 Born where? _____

3 Address? _____

4 School? (use *go to*) _____

5 Year? _____

6 Hobbies? _____

7 Languages? How long learning? 1 _____

   since _____

   2 _____

   since _____

8 Skills? (use *can*)   1 _____

   2 _____

9 Qualifications? _____

_____

10 Work experience? _____

   since _____

Writing Tip

When you write a letter of application, ask questions about the job.
It shows that you are really interested in the job.

5 Write questions about a holiday job that would interest you.
Possible question words: *Where? How long? How much?*

Putting sentences together

6 Write sentences together with *in* or *since.*

Examples:
I/born/London

I was born in London.
I/use/computer/1998

I've been using a computer since 1998.

1 I/use/Word 7/at home and at school/2000
2 I/born/1989
3 I/learn/English/1999
4 I/help/my father's shop/2000
5 I/coach/young swimmers/1998

Writing Tip

To write a CV and a holiday job application follow the models and
put in new information about yourself and the job you want.

7 Write a CV and a job application for a holiday job that interests you. If you
want to, you can put the CV and the job application on computer.

Writing argument and opinion

Completing sentences

1 **Look at the types of TV programme. Then complete the sentences. Has your partner got the same ideas?**

sports programmes, current affairs/news programmes, drama series, comedy series, programmes for teenagers, cartoons, films

There should be more _____ on TV.

I think there are too many _____ on TV.

In my opinion, there shouldn't be any _____ on TV.

2 **Fill in gaps 1–8 with a–g.**

a Yes, I really love old black

b It seems to me that a lot of cartoons

c I think there should be more

d Why aren't there more films on TV

e Yes, why isn't it on every

f I like cartoons with no

g I think programmes about doctors

h In my opinion, there are too many

1 _____ _____ football on TV.

2 _____ _____ Saturday?

3 _____ _____ series about hospitals.

4 _____ _____ and nurses are exciting.

5 _____ _____ are silly.

6 _____ _____ violence.

7 _____ _____ like this one?

8 _____ _____ and white films.

3 Complete the sentences.

1 I would like to see more programmes like _____ on TV.

2 My favourite programme on TV is _____ because

_____ .

3 It seems to me that programmes like _____ are bad because

_____ .

4 In my opinion, programmes like _____ are good because

_____ .

Writing sentences

4 **The English in these opinions is correct, but write them again so that they make sense.**

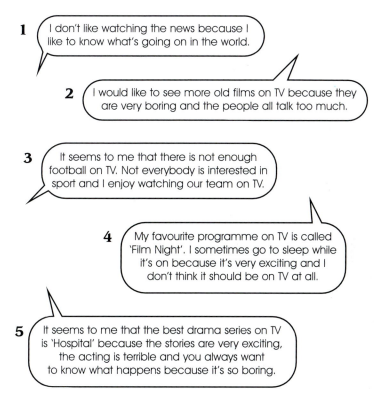

1   I don't like watching the news because I like to know what's going on in the world.

2   I would like to see more old films on TV because they are very boring and the people all talk too much.

3   It seems to me that there is not enough football on TV. Not everybody is interested in sport and I enjoy watching our team on TV.

4   My favourite programme on TV is called 'Film Night'. I sometimes go to sleep while it's on because it's very exciting and I don't think it should be on TV at all.

5   It seems to me that the best drama series on TV is 'Hospital' because the stories are very exciting, the acting is terrible and you always want to know what happens because it's so boring.

Example:

1 I like watching the news because I like to know what's going on in the world.

5 **Use these questions to write argument and opinion sentences about programmes you watch on TV.**

Example: I think that 'Hospital' is a very good drama series because the acting is good and the stories are exciting and believable.

1 Is the acting good and are the stories exciting and believable?

2 Is your favourite team on often enough and do they show some good foreign teams?

3 Does it keep you up to date about what is going on in your country?

4 Does it make you laugh because the people do silly things?

Putting sentences together

6 **Write these statements as argument and opinion sentences, using the word or words in brackets.**

Example: There is too much football on TV (opinion)

In my opinion there is too much football on TV.

1 The news is the best programme on TV at the moment. (think)

2 This is an excellent drama series with good acting. (seems)

3 There are programmes made specially for teenagers. (should)

4 There are a lot of programmes like this. (should, more)

5 This is a really excellent sports programme. (would, see, more)

7 **Plan your perfect evening of TV programmes and say why you like each programme. Then plan the worst evening of TV that you can imagine and say why you don't like each programme. You can use real programmes or you can imagine them.**

⋈ Plan the two evenings of programmes – good and bad.

⋈ Write the start and finish time of each programme.

⋈ Say what each programme is, for example, 'Drama series in a hospital'.

⋈ Write your opinion of each programme.

⋈ Write 'general' opinions using this programme as an example, for example, 'There should be more programmes on TV for teenagers like this one.'

⋈ Show your work to other people in the class. Have they got the same ideas as you?

Writing about future hopes

Completing sentences

1 Work with a partner. What jobs do you think people in your class might have in ten years' time? Discuss this and write some of your opinions.

Example: I think John might be an engineer.

_____

2 Complete the sentences about yourself with *I hope to*, *I might* or *I might not*.

In ten years' time …

1 _____ have a good job.

2 _____ get married and have a family of my own.

3 _____ be in another country.

4 _____ be very different from the person I am now.

5 _____ be a(n) _____ .

6 _____ be able to _____ .

7 _____ buy myself a _____ .

8 _____ have these hobbies: _____ .

3 Complete the sentences. Describe yourself in ten years' time.

1 I might be _____ tall.

2 I might weigh _____ .

3 My hair might _____ .

4 Most of the time I think I might wear

_____ .

5 But for parties I might wear

_____ .

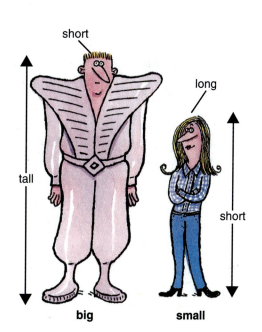

Writing sentences

4 Robert is imagining what he might do when he grows up. Write sentences about Robert.

might/live

want/work

might/work

want/help

might/live

might/commute

1 _____ Robert might live on the Moon. _____

2 _____

3 _____

4 _____

5 _____

6 _____

5 Use the cues to write sentences comparing your life in ten years' time to your life now.

Example: get up – earlier or later?

     In ten years' time I might get up later than I get up now.

1 work – harder or less hard?

2 watch TV – more or less?

3 use a computer – more or less?

4 speak English – more often or less often?

5 have free time – more or less?

Putting sentences together

6 Write the two sentences again as one using *hope to* + *when* or *in*.

Example: Be a doctor. Ten years' time.

I hope to be a doctor in ten years' time.
Be a doctor. Leave school.

I hope to be a doctor when I leave school.

1 Be rich and happy. A few years' time.
2 Stay in this country. Have my own family.
3 Go on holiday. A few months' time.
4 Get a car. I'm old enough.
5 Get a car. A few years' time.

7 Write a paragraph about your future hopes in ten years' time. Use expressions like *hope to*, *might* and *might not*.

✄ Describe how you might look in ten years' time.
✄ Describe the family you hope for in ten years' time.
✄ Describe the work you hope to do in ten years' time.
✄ Talk about the hobbies you hope to have in ten years' time.

Writing Tip

Plan what you want to say before you start writing. Make notes about what you want to say and then write the paragraph from your notes.

Pearson Education Limited
Edinburgh Gate
Harlow
Essex CM20 2JE
England

and Associated Companies throughout the world

www.longman-elt.com

First published 2000

ISBN 0582 41962 X

Set in Avant Garde and Leawood Infant.

Printed in Lebanon by Librairie du Liban.

Prepared for the publishers by Gecko Limited, Granville Way, Bicester,
Oxfordshire OX6 0JT.

Acknowledgements
We are grateful to the following for permission to reproduce photographs:
Bruce Coleman Collection/John Visser for 6 bottom right; Ronald Grant Archive for 26,
38 bottom left; NHPA/Daniel Heuclin for 6 top left; Oxford Scientific Films/David B
Fleetham for 5; Popperfoto for 17 top (Bob Thomas), 17 middle, 17 bottom (PPP);
Sporting Pictures (UK) Ltd for 32, 38 top left; Stone for 6 top right (Jeff Rotman), 6
bottom left (Daniel J Cox), 38 top right (Bruce Ayres); Warner Bros/First National (courtesy
Kobal) for 38 bottom right.

Illustrations by Peter Richardson, Andy Quelch, Chris Brown, Kath Walker and
Gecko Limited.

With special thanks to Lewis Lansford for his contribution as Freelance Project Manager.